STORMS FROM THE SKY

LAKSHMI JAHNAVI

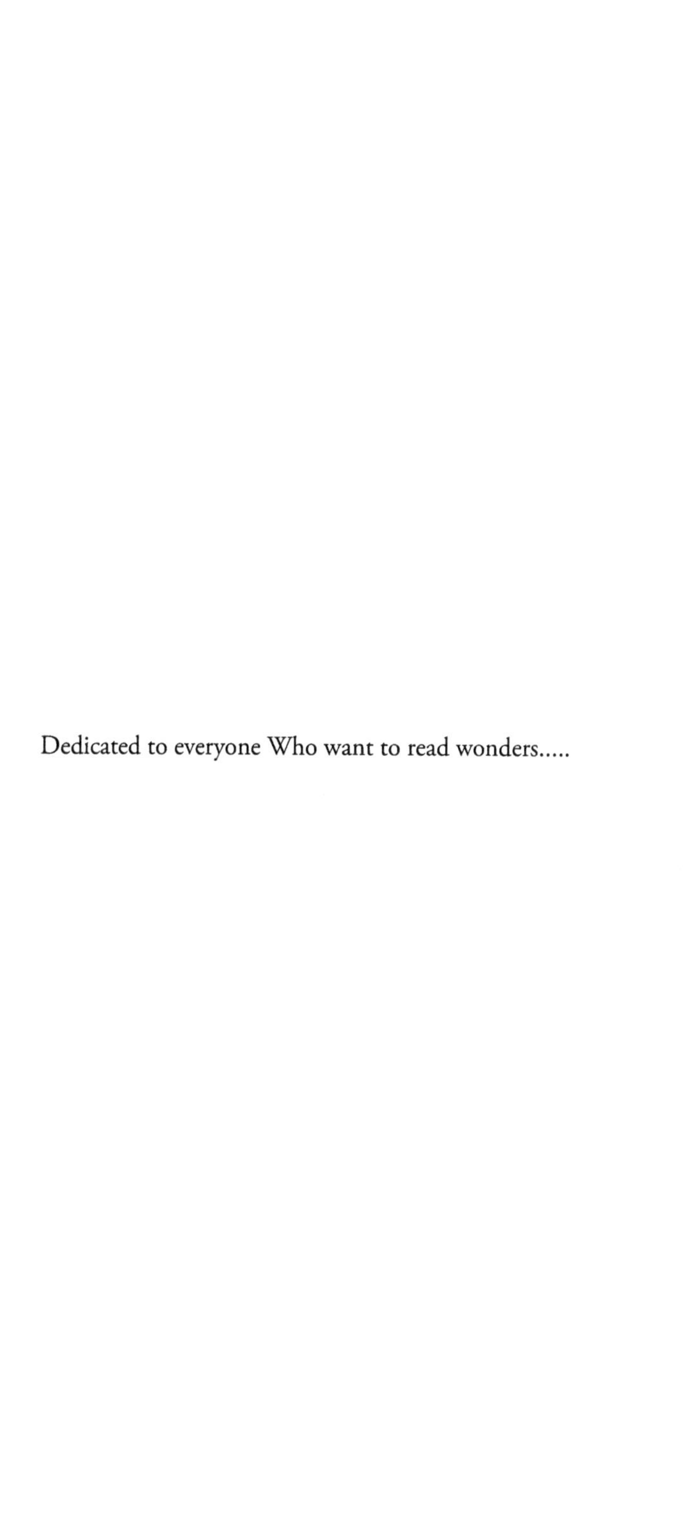

Dedicated to everyone Who want to read wonders.....

Contents

Foreword	*vii*
Preface	*ix*
Acknowledgements	*xi*
Prologue	*xiii*
Authors Bio	*xv*
Content	*xvii*
1. Disturbance	1
2. Fidelity	2
3. Encouragement	3
4. Love	5
5. Adore	6
6. Zeal	7
7. Life	8
8. My Dear	10
9. Admiration	11
10. Friendship	12
11. Purity	14
12. Appreciation	15
13. Unknown Sensations	17
14. My Acceptance	18
15. Its You	19
16. Hope	20
17. Pressures	21
18. Grief	22

Contents

19. Waiting For The Dearest 23

20. Missed Soul 25

21. Arbitrary Emotions 26

22. Cautiosness 27

23. Random Sunset Thoughts 28

24. A Peacefull Desire 30

25. Conscience 32

26. Acceptance 33

27. Emotions 35

28. You To Me 37

Foreword

THE FLOW OF WRITING BEGIN................

Preface

Words build AUTHORS...

Books Attracts Reader...

Feel The Words...

This is an Anthology book...

We formed the basic idea of an anthology and soon worked on it.

it took some time..

later i found all the poems and made them in order...

The editing part is done by a young girl Harika...

The book is dedicated to all the reader.

The motivation to publish this book was

given by the situation and circumstances of life....

Every poem in this book has a great feel.

it reaches the reader life....

it attracts the reader soul.

Acknowledgements

I would like to thank my mother and father for the super support.I am grateful to Mr sharma for his motivation and support.He has been a great support for everytime in my work.A special thanks to MS HARIKA for helping me in all the aspects.They all kept me going this book would not have been possible without these...
jai mata di......

Prologue

THIS BOOK IS BASICALLY AN ANTOLOGY............

Authors Bio

Lakshmi jahnavi

Lakshmi jahnavi is a determined courageous teen writer. Writing is not just an escape but her passion. Started writing at 12, and to date finished 300+ writeups on vivid topics. She believes that writing is an art that comes from the heart. Her pen is just the means of communicating her emotions. Her works are not restricted to a particular genre and never fail to impress the readers. Some of her admirable poems are presented in "Colourless canvas".Her writings are a waterfall of consciousness flowing with pebbles of emotions and life experiences.

Content

a. Preface
b. The author
1. Disturbance
2. Fidelity
3. Encouragement
4. Love
5. Adore
6. Zeal
7. Life
8. My dear
9. Admiration
10. Friendship
11. Purity
12. Appreciation
13. Unknown sensations
14. My acceptance
15. It's you
16. Hope
17. Pressures
18. Grief
19. Waiting for the dearest
20. Missed soul
21. Arbitrary emotions
22. Cautiousness
23. Random sunset thoughts
24. A peaceful desire
25. Conscience
26. Acceptance
27. Emotions
28. You to me

1. DISTURBANCE

The disturbance is a thing that everyone feels in life. The disturbance is interestless of one in situations.
Some situations disturb us very much because we don't want those to happen in life.
Disturbing situations are the most common thing that happens in all our lives.

But it is necessary to overcome those disturbances and make sure that those disturbances should not lead our lives. I agree it's not in our hands.
But withstanding that disturbance is important.

2. FIDELITY

Sometimes love stories don't have happy endings...

Proud of his death and sad to his death kills her...

Remembering the great heroes, brave legends of India for their courageous sacrifice

Their sacrifice is incomparable.....

3. ENCOURAGEMENT

The motive to do something is a wonderful thing. And the pressure of someone to do something is a very dominant thing in one's own life.

"Encouraging one to do something is like giving sweetness to the tasteless fruit"...........

Encouraging gives zeel and excitement to the one. And it's like giving support like a stick for a plant.

You may not remember the one who you encouraged but the one who was encouraged by you will remember you...

"Encourage even an ant to climb a hill".The one who encourages is always a hero because the one who left the bledy jealous can only do that.

Be a supporter but not a foolish discourager. "Encouragement can give fresh air in the polluted environment. " "Jealous should not be the answer to discouragement."

4. LOVE

I shower in the rain of your love.....
I bloom like a flower in the season of your care.....
I dance like a peacock in the rain called your possessiveness...
I sing like a cuckoo on the tree called your heart......
Thank you so much for giving comfortable space in your heart by adjusting your blood capillaries...

Let's be together and forever...

5. ADORE

The sparkles of your love sprinkling in my eyes ...
I don't need any explanations for the quantity of love you have for me,
because I hope I know you.
And that is rising like a sun in the direction of you and it doesn't know how to set.......

The care you show towards me giving wings to me to fly in the sky is called love.....

And you are my everything and anything...

6. ZEAL

The zeal to know something is always great. That curiosity to know or to learn is something special.

A new power will always travel with us in that zeal. And that power gives them the confidence to learn more.

In that zeel Man finds himself.
The power which comes from that zeal is never replaceable.

And that zeal and curiousness are important to one's own life.
As it changes life.
The specialty of life starts with the zeal to learn something or anything...

7. LIFE

Life is a mystery,
We can't able to describe life.
In this mysterious life of some years
What we will find?
What is the use of this life?
How complicated is life?
How wonderful is life?

We crawl,
We walk,
We run...

How wonderful life is, it teaches us to crawl-walk-run, and again rest.

With the two tiny eyes, we can see the vast world...
What about this small heart
How many feel it should feel??

We are the wonderful creatures
Because we see wonders in each stage of life.

No one is useless,
No one is helpless
Life itself helps you,

Make wonders,
Feel wonders,

Live life in a fascinating way......

8. MY DEAR

Your eyes represent my vision,
Your heart became my habitat,
Your soul became my kingdom,
Your possessiveness became my
solider,
Your lap became my cushion,
Your love became my world,
Your smile became my touch,
Your promises became my blessings,
Your sorrow becomes my curse,
You are my boon,
And
I hope I will withstand that boon.

9. ADMIRATION

The admiration of beauty starts with the feeling that we look at Beauty...
That feeling is something great, we that feel we can feel the beauties...

Sometimes, a consistent sky may appear beautiful... It's not the sky that designed itself for some time. But it's the way of feeling and looking towards the sky.......

And that feeling makes the usual things look beautiful.

"It's not the things that appear beautiful, it's the feeling that makes to look beautiful is beautiful"

10. FRIENDSHIP

A friend writing a note on
her best friend.....

A tiny fatty friend who is warm to hug,
hot to see, easy to quarrel and win is
you. "You came to my world and
introduced another world called
friendship".

You are my fatty and hottie,
I love to quarrel with you always.
You are earth in my world so that I can
stamp you always.

In my little world, you took large space
because I know you need more space
to settle.

"Friendship is magic.
And you became the magician".
I hope you became the strength to a
poor heart.

People come and go in lives but to
withstand one's connection with the
bonds of trust and purity is important.

I hope we withstand the relationship
called friendship.

11. PURITY

Purity is a huge word,
It is a large expression.
We are losing purity in our lives.
I accept we commit mistakes,
We commit wrongs in our lives but
those don't distract purity.

Purity is trustworthiness and being completely involved in things and being original.

It doesn't state the do's
and don'ts.
It just states completeness and
trustworthiness.

Originality and trustworthiness are the roots of purity.

12. APPRECIATION

Sometimes we need appreciation in our lives, not to feel proud but to do proud things.

The right appreciation from loved ones is always special and pushes us to do something big.
Huge magic in life starts with tiny beginnings.

Appreciation sometimes encourages us to do something great in our lives. We sometimes don't know the destination and we should not even search for it. We should flow like a water sometimes.

After flowing like a water we should bloom like a flower and after blooming we should light like a sun. We don't know how it started and we don't know how it's gonna be ended.

I hope, once started it doesn't gonna end. Because it's not homework to start and finish.
It's life and it is eternal.

13. UNKNOWN SENSATIONS

Not knowing what to do but some curiosity inside to do something kills.

Life always puts in difficult times. But not interested to quit life.

But not interested to look at bad circumstances always in life.

Not knowing what is happening.
But something is going on in life...
What happens........
What's going..........
What changes.......

Let's leave it for destiny this time.

14. MY ACCEPTANCE

The peace that I achieved from taking a decision is unexplainable.

This peace is something different and teaches me to stand on that decision.

Encouraging to stand on that decision.
The relief and peace are something special.

Some hate my decision,
Some accept my decision,
Whatever it is,
That's mine and no one has the right to judge it.

My life,
My decision,
My acceptance.............

15. ITS YOU

I don't know what is life like.....
I don't know how to live...
I don't know anything...
Just living, but not satisfied with my life.

You came to my life like a moon in the dark.
You learned me how to live,
You learned me to discover...

I was hesitant about my life and you made my life very interesting...

Because I don't know that You are my life until you come to my life...

16. HOPE

A happy leading life has many turns. Every turn is edging spines and every spine is hurting brutally.....

And, every hurt is taking its route to sorrow and pain.

Hoping to have turns with smooth edging.

17. PRESSURES

The experience of lightest part of life starts with the patience and peace you shown towards the things....

Taking things as issues or pressures always put us in trouble.

We can't get solutions in that pressure. As we can't see sky when it is raining ,we only see sky when it is clear and calm..

Our brain doesn't show solutions when it is pressured.
Patience itself helps us...

Don't let your pressures lead you...

18. GRIEF

Falling from the hill of pain to the depths of sorrow........

But feeling the fall,
Feeling the breeze of hurt,
Looking into the waves of grief,

After fallen,
Now I am drowning in the sea called sorrow,
I just don't want to come back to that pain,
No options,
Staying in sorrow is the only option.

But suddenly I noticed a boat of happiness is coming to me...

Will it reach me?????

Hoping it also should not drown in the sea called sorrow !!!

19. WAITING FOR THE DEAREST

Waiting for the dearest,

Waiting to meet you,
Waiting to stay happy,
Waiting to smile heartfully,
Waiting to go along with you,
Waiting to feel happiness,
Waiting to go deep down with you,
Waiting for you.....

My dearest good time
Please come soon

I'm tired to be of bad times,

My dearest good time come sooner your presence is what I need.........

20. MISSED SOUL

That name you called me is roaring in
my ears.
But this time it's not you, it's just my inner
imagination.
It's foolishness to stare at you again
even after you left the me..........

21. ARBITRARY EMOTIONS

Seeing stars from my window
And my eyes started watering
I don't know why......
But the way the stars are shining in
their light in dark is all inspiring
me.........
I don't know what's going on in my
mind...
The sounds of insects are like saying
good night to me...
The way the breeze is coming is very
soothing
Life is incomplete without mysteries.....

But we drown in some moments we
don't even WHY??

22. CAUTIOSNESS

Cautiousness is very important in one's own life...
Life is unpredictable anything can happen at any time
But being cautious is another level of living...
We can't imagine some situations in our lives...
But, cautiousness plays a crucial role in our lives...

Cautiousness may sometimes be the reason for no problem...
Cautiousness is the major effect that lives deeply settle...

Live cautiously.........

23. RANDOM SUNSET THOUGHTS

Not finding words to write...
But finding feelings to write...

One sunset with a pleasant heart is
enough to find a million words...

Words are not mandatory...
But feelings are...

Because not all words describe
feelings...
Some feelings are beautiful and we
exactly don't know what they are called...

Getting chased by feelings...
Running, running running running but I'm
not able to escape...

Finally caught in millions of feelings...

I don't know what name I have to give to
that feeling...

24. A PEACEFULL DESIRE

I need regular refreshments in life...

I don't say I want happiness...
I am just asking life to give some space and a new bang refreshment.....

Asking for refreshments, not for a fresh start but also a fresh stop...

It became a need...

To push life forward and to pull our souls from falling back...

Need a refreshment like a bang with no worries, no emotional dramas, no problems,   only just comfort ness, and smiling faces till the end...

I don't know whether my heart relaxes or not in that comfort ness??!!!..

Hoping for a bang refreshment that refreshes my heart...

25. CONSCIENCE

Many reasons are holding me back to stay in the past.
But my inner voice is motivating me to go forward, to a life where there are no past regrets, and moving forward is the only option now.

Life is full of thorns, it's our responsibility to protect our body and soul from thorns.
Because some thorns deeply attack the souls.

And life is also full of flowers too.
It's our responsibility to choose a nice flower that appears good and has medicinal value, has a nice fragrance
Because appearance may cheat us from picking the exact one.....

26. ACCEPTANCE

Putting pressure towards things to
accept is a foolish thing that you do to a
person.
Because his /her preference is huge.
You don't have trust that they can get
that huge thing.

But their belief and soulfull trust on that
huge thing is never explainable.

Let us leave them now and society
should give them a chance to do
big.......

Change your mindset to do big things.
Because a wolf don't kill a mice for his
hunger.

Think big, do big.

Don't buy a moon for lighting a
room ....

Big things need big mind I hope you
have it...

Burn,
Rise,
Light...

27. EMOTIONS

Sometimes we feel low...
Sometimes we feel high...
Sometimes we feel why??
Sometimes we feel shy.....
Sometimes we feel to fly...
Sometimes we feel too cry...
Sometimes we feel to try.....
Sometimes we feel to die......

Every feeling is a wonder in life.
We should not feel weird or guilty about feelings.

Sixty years of life can show sixty thousand feelings...

Feel all the feelings in life don't feel guilty to feel feelings. Only we humans can feel feelings ...

Life is very little,
Enjoy all the feelings,
Share all your feelings...
Feel every situation.

28. YOU TO ME

YOU CAME INTO MY LIFE.
YOU DEFINED MY LIFE.
YOU GAVE ME LIFE.
YOU BECAME MY LIFE.

THANK YOU

Printed by Libri Plureos GmbH in Hamburg,
Germany